W9-AWT-721

LIGHT

experimenting with science

Antonella Meiani

Lerner Publications Company • Minneapolis

First American edition published in 2003 by Lerner Publications Company

Published by arrangement with Istituto Geografico DeAgostini, Novara, Italy

Originally published as *Il Grande Libro degli Esperimenti*

Copyright © 1999 by Istituto Geografico DeAgostini, Novara, Italy

Translated from the Italian by Maureen Spurgeon.
Translation copyright © 2000 by Brown Watson, England.

This book has been adapted from a single-volume work entitled *Il Grande Libro degli Esperimenti*, originally published by Istituto Geografico DeAgostini, Novara, Italy, in 1999. New back matter was developed by Lerner Publications Company.

Lerner Publications Company
A division of Lerner Publishing Group
241 First Avenue North
Minneapolis, MN 55401 U.S.A.

Website address: www.lernerbooks.com

Library of Congress Cataloging-in-Publication Data

Meiani, Antonella.
    [Grande libro degli esperimenti. English. Selections]
    Light / by Antonella Meiani—1st American ed.
        p.   cm. — (Experimenting with science)
    Includes bibliographical references and index.
    Summary: Experiments with light explain shadows and colors, and demonstrate such concepts as reflection and refraction.
        ISBN: 0–8225–0084–1 (lib. bdg. : alk. paper)
        1. Light—Experiments—Juvenile literature. [1. Light—Experiments. 2. Experiments.]
    I. Title.
    QC360.M4413 2003
    535'.078—dc21   2001038947

Manufactured in the United States of America
1 2 3 4 5 6 – JR – 08 07 06 05 04 03

Table of Contents

4

Light

How do shadows form? Why does light enable us to see? How do lenses work? How do our eyes see things?
Find the answers to these and many more questions by doing the experiments in the following pages, under these headings:

- Rays of light
- Reflection
- Refraction
- Colors
- Capturing an image

Rays of light

Nothing in the universe is faster than the speed of light. It travels at the extraordinary rate of 300,000 km (186,000 mi.) per second! But how does light travel from its source (whether this source is the Sun or a lamp) to the object on which it shines? Can light illuminate all the sides of an object? What exactly are shadows? How are shadows made? Can they change shape?

To answer these questions, we must discover some facts about light, finding out where it comes from, which things stop light from traveling, and which things it can shine through.

How does light spread?

A STRAIGHT PATH

You need:
- two squares of cardboard
- flashlight
- two strips of cardboard
- a few thick books

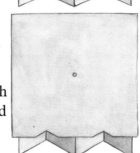

What to do:

1 Poke a hole in the center of each of the two cardboard squares. Make supports for each square by folding the cardboard strips and cutting notches, as you see in the picture.

2 Place the squares in the supports and line up the holes. Put the flashlight on the books, with the light aimed at the hole in the first square. Kneel or sit down so that your eyes are level with the hole in the second square.

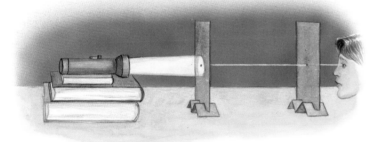

What happens?
Your eye sees the light through the two holes.

3 Move one of the squares so that the holes are no longer lined up.

What happens?
Your eye can no longer see the light.

Why?
Light travels in a straight line, so it cannot pass through the hole if the hole is not in its path.

A LIGHT ON THE WORLD

You need:
- globe
- portable lamp
- darkened room

What to do:

1 Point the lamp directly at the globe.

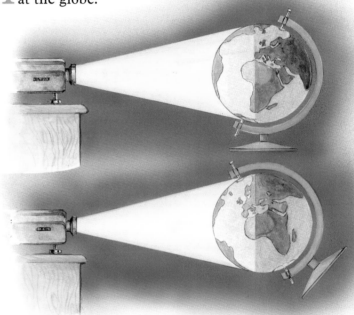

2 Move the globe up and down, then side to side, keeping it in the light.

What happens?
Only the part of the globe that is turned toward the source of light is illuminated. The opposite side always remains in the dark, no matter how you hold it.

Why?
The rays of light follow a straight path. They cannot curve around an object and light up the side that cannot be seen. That is why the Sun can only shine on one side of Earth, the side that is turned toward its rays. On the side of Earth facing away from the Sun, there is darkness.

Light travels in straight lines. If something blocks its path, it can only illuminate the part of the object that is facing it.

What causes shadows?

STOP THE LIGHT

You need:
- flashlight
- table lamp
- piece of black cardboard
- scissors
- tape
- stick
- darkened room

What to do:

1 Cut the black cardboard into whatever shape you like. Tape the black shape onto the stick.

2 Hold the shape between the beam of the flashlight and the wall of the room.

3 First, bring the shape nearer to the light, then move it back towards the wall.

What happens?
The closer the shape is to the flashlight, the bigger the shadow on the wall. The farther the shape is from the flashlight, the smaller the shadow.

Why?
When an object blocks the straight path of the light, a shadow forms behind that object. The closer the object is to the source of the light, the more light it blocks out, so its shadow is bigger. But if the object is farther away, it does not block out as much light, so the shadow is smaller.

4 Now shine the table lamp on the shape.

What happens?
The shadow's outline is more blurred than before.

Why?
When the source of light is bigger than the object, the shadow that forms is dark at the center and lighter towards the edges, where only part of the light can reach. The darkest part of the shadow is called the umbra. The area of light shadow is called the penumbra.

When the Sun, Moon, and Earth are in a straight line, there is an eclipse, where the Sun or Moon is wholly or partly hidden. When the Moon is between Earth and the Sun, this is a solar eclipse. If Earth comes between the Sun and Moon, this is a lunar eclipse.

A GARDEN SUNDIAL

You need:
- cardboard disc, about 20 cm (8 in.) in diameter
- stick about 10–15cm (4–6 in.) long
- scissors
- pencil
- watch
- patch of ground where the Sun shines through-out the day

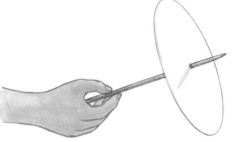

What to do:

1 Make a hole in the center of the disc. Push the stick through, to about one-third of its length. Push the stick into the ground so that the disc is firmly on the ground.

2 As soon as your watch is on the hour, mark where the shadow of the stick falls on the disc. Write down the time beside the line.

3 Do the same thing each hour, remembering to write down the time for each shadow.

What happens?
The shadow cast by the stick is in a different position each hour. The pencil lines spread out from the stick toward the outer edge of the disc.

Why?
The position of the stick's shadow changes as the position of the Sun appears to change. What really happens is that Earth is rotating at a constant speed, either toward the Sun or away from it.

You have made a sundial, an instrument once used for the measurement of time. Sundials can still be seen today on the walls of some old houses and in the grounds of ancient squares and gardens.

In the shadow of a tree

Within the space of one day, the position of the Sun in relation to Earth changes. (This is because Earth is rotating on its axis.) Therefore, the direction of the Sun's rays also changes. That is why shadows "move." When the Sun is high, it throws short shadows. When it is low on the horizon, the shadows are longer.

When an object blocks out light, it casts a shadow, which is an area where the rays of light cannot reach.

Do all objects cast shadows?

TO PASS OR NOT TO PASS?

You need:
- flashlight
- book
- cup
- glass with some water
- piece of thin glass
- piece of thin paper
- handkerchief
- piece of tissue paper
- darkened room

What to do:
1 Line up the objects in front of a wall. Shine the flashlight on each of them in turn.

What happens?
Shadows form on the wall behind the cup and the book. Behind the glass and the sheet of glass, the wall is lit up. There is a blurred halo behind the tissue paper, the piece of paper, and the handkerchief.

Why?
The cup and the book are *opaque* (cannot be seen through) and so these objects stop light. The thin piece of glass and the water are *transparent* (can be seen through). Materials like the thin paper, the tissue paper, and the handkerchief are *translucent* (let some light through). So they only partially block out the rays of light. The light that remains spreads out to illuminate the wall slightly.

A halo around the Moon
The atmosphere around Earth can become translucent. When crystals of ice form on high parts of Earth's surface, they spread out the light that is reflected from the Moon. They reflect the light back, making it look as if there is a halo around the Moon.

THE TRANSPARENT EFFECT

You need:
- sheet of paper
- drops of oil
- drinking straw
- flashlight
- darkened room

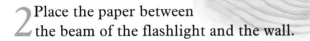

What to do:

1 Use the straw to shake one or two drops of oil onto the paper.

2 Place the paper between the beam of the flashlight and the wall.

3 Switch on the flashlight. Shine the light on the oily patch.

What happens?
When you shine the flashlight on the oily patch, the light passes through it to the wall and it is much stronger.

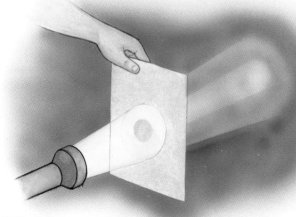

Why?
The paper blocks out many of the light rays. The oil penetrates through the fibers of the paper, making little transparent holes that allow the light to pass through. The same thing does not happen with water, because it cannot as easily penetrate the fibers of most types of paper.

Why can we see through some materials?

The eye is equipped to see things in light. If there is a transparent material (for example, a pane of glass or a shop window, or even a small quantity of water) between the eye and the object in the light, then we can see the object perfectly.

However, it is not only the type of material that lets the light pass through or blocks it out, but also the thickness of that material. For example, although water in a glass is transparent, deep water in the sea is not. In the same way, glass that is just a few millimeters thick is transparent, but glass that is several meters thick is not.

Translucent materials, those that let only a certain amount of light pass through, allow us to make out only the shape of objects. Through a curtain or paper, for instance, we see only vague shapes.

Only opaque objects block out rays of light and cast shadows.

Reflection

Why is it not possible to see anything in the dark? How can the Sun shine on everything that surrounds us?

To see, our eyes use the way that light rays reflect when those rays strike an object that is not transparent. We see everything that is struck by rays of light because our eyes use the light reflected from things. And if we can receive those reflected rays well enough, we can make images that are identical to the real thing.

How does light allow us to see things?

SHINING WHITE

You need:
- sheet of white paper
- sheet of black paper
- flashlight
- mirror
- darkened room

What to do:

1 Switch on the flashlight in a darkened room and stand in front of a mirror.

2 Hold the flashlight sideways to your face, so that the light shines on your nose.

3 Using your free hand, hold the black paper beside your face so the light shines on it. How does this change your reflection in the mirror? Do the same with the white paper.

What happens?
The flashlight by itself lights up only your nose. If you hold up the black paper, the reflection of your face is almost completely hidden. With the white paper, almost your whole face is illuminated.

Why?
With the flashlight alone, the light reflects back only from the object it meets, which is your nose. With the paper, the effect depends on the color. The black paper reflects only a bit of the light that shines on it. But the white paper reflects a lot of the light. These rays of light reflect back onto your face, illuminating it.

FROM THE DARK INTO THE LIGHT

You need:
- a darkened room full of different objects (a storeroom, for example)

What to do:

1 Go into the darkened room. Close the door and look around.

2 Open the door a little so that there is only a tiny crack to let in light. Look around again. Gradually open the door more, until it is open wide.

What happens?

When the door is closed, your eyes cannot see the objects in the room. With the first shafts of light, you begin to distinguish the objects a little more. Gradually, as more light enters, you see all the objects clearly.

Why?

Things are visible only when they reflect light—that is, when light is sent back to our eyes. Pale objects reflect a lot of light. Darker objects absorb a great deal of light, so they reflect only a little. We need a lot of light to see darker objects.

We see objects only if rays of light strike them, bounce off, and then return to our eyes.

How do mirrors work?

TRUE REFLECTIONS

You need:
- piece of stiff black cardboard
- small square or rectangular mirror
- scissors
- flashlight
- darkened room

What to do:

1 Fold the piece of cardboard, as shown in the picture. Then cut three slots along one side.

2 In the darkened room, switch on the flashlight and place it behind the slots.

3 Place the mirror at the opposite side of the folded cardboard, as shown in the picture.

What happens?
When the rays of light strike the mirror, each ray bounces back at an angle.

Why?
The mirror reflects the light with the angle of reflection the same as the angle with which the ray strikes the mirror (angle of incidence). If a ray of light strikes the reflective surface in a perpendicular (straight on) direction, it reflects back along the same path. If a surface is smooth, all of the reflected rays go in the same direction. If the surface is rough, the rays bounce back in many different directions.

MIRROR AGAINST MIRROR

You need:
- two flat mirrors

What to do:

1 Look into a mirror and move your hand.

What happens?
Your reflection is shown in reverse—if you move your right hand, it will look like your left hand in the mirror.

2 Place the two mirrors on a table at an angle to each other. Sit in front of them.

3 Move your hand.

What happens?
Your reflection is now correct. When you move your right hand, your right hand moves in the reflection.

Why?
When the reflected light from your body strikes a mirror in front of you, it bounces straight back, creating the reversed image. But when you face two mirrors, each mirror reverses the reversed reflection from the other, and the reflection is "straightened out"!

MAKE A PERISCOPE

You need:
- piece of strong cardboard, 28 cm × 43 cm (11 × 17 in.)
- scissors
- tape
- two rectangular mirrors, 6 cm × 10 cm (2 × 4 in.)
- ruler
- pencil
- two pieces of cardboard, each 6 cm (2 in.) square

What to do:

1 Using the ruler, divide the cardboard into four equal parts, each 7 cm (2¾ in.) wide. Draw two 5-cm (2-in.) squares as shown in the picture. Cut these squares out.

2 Cut one of the 6-cm (2 in.) squares in half diagonally to make two right-angled triangles.

3 Place one of the triangles on the top strip of the paper, as shown in the picture. Draw along the diagonal line, then cut along it to make a slit. Do this again in the three other places shown in the picture. Fold the cardboard along the long lines to make a tube. Join the sides with tape.

4 Thread the two mirrors through the slits. You have made a periscope.

5 Get behind an obstacle (such as a wall or a windowsill) so that the periscope is sticking up above your head. Look through the square at the bottom.

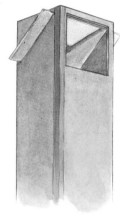

What happens?
In the mirror inside the periscope, you will see a reflected image of whatever is on the other side of the obstacle.

Why?
The light that reflects from the objects or people on the other side of the obstacle strikes the mirror at the top of the periscope. Because of the angle of this mirror, it is also reflected in the bottom mirror. You can use your periscope to look at something without being seen—just like submarine crews who need to survey the sea before coming up to the surface!

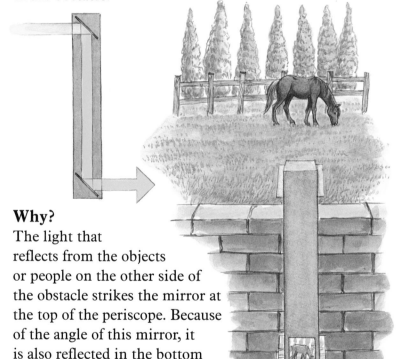

Mirrors reflect light and reproduce the images of things facing them.

Can light bend?

LIGHT BOUNCES BACK

You need:
- see-through container with flat sides
- water
- a few drops of milk
- flashlight
- piece of black cardboard
- scissors
- tape
- thick book
- darkened room

What to do:

1 Fill the container with water and add a few drops of milk. (This makes the rays of light easier to see.)

2 Poke a hole in the middle of the black cardboard. Then tape it over the lens of the flashlight.

3 In a darkened room, switch on the flashlight and shine it as you see in the picture, so that the beam of light goes through the water toward its surface. (You may find it helps to put the container on a thick book.)

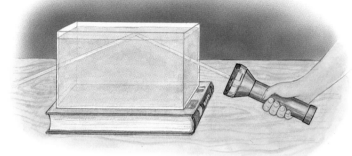

What happens?
When it strikes the surface of the water, the light bends and goes out of the container from the opposite side so that the beam forms an angle.

Why?
Light enters the container along a straight path. The surface of the water works like a mirror and reflects the light. This reflection alters the path of the light, which, in order to stay straight, changes direction.

Lasers
A laser beam is a very intense and fine ray of light that carries an enormous amount of energy. To make a laser, light is produced by special procedures and is then reflected back and forth between a pair of mirrors to increase the intensity. When it reaches the intensity required, the laser beam passes through one of the mirrors, which is only partly reflective. Because of its power, its precision, and the fact that it can be controlled easily, lasers are used in numerous fields—cutting materials (from lengths of fabric to sheets of steel), joining metal parts together, making precise measurements, performing surgical operations, creating special effects, producing and playing compact discs, producing and reading bar codes for products on sale in shops, and many other purposes.

A LUMINOUS JET

You need:
- clear, soft plastic bottle
- piece of thin, clear plastic tubing
- bowl
- modeling clay
- tape
- thick, dark cloth
- darkened room
- water
- scissors
- flashlight

What to do:

1 Fill the bottle with water.

2 Ask an adult to use the scissors to make a hole in the cap of the bottle. Thread the tubing inside, holding it in place with modeling clay.

3 Tape the flashlight at the bottom of the bottle. Switch on the flashlight. Wrap the whole thing in the cloth, leaving only the tubing uncovered.

4 In a dark room, place the bottle so that a jet of water can be poured smoothly through the tubing and into the bowl.

What happens?
A jet of luminous water comes out of the bottle.

Why?
The light follows the path of water through the curving tube. Inside this tube, the light cannot bend but is constantly reflected against the walls of the tubing, proceeding in a zig-zag direction because it is trapped inside. This phenomenon is called total internal reflection.

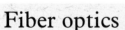

Fiber optics

Optical fibers are very thin, transparent filaments. Light enters at one end and escapes through the other. By the effect of total internal reflection, the light stays trapped on the inside and becomes bent by the filament. Fiber optics are used to examine the human body. Because of the fibers' flexibility and their fine dimensions, they can reach many parts of the body (such as the stomach and the arteries), illuminating these parts and sending back an image for a doctor to see by looking through a lens outside the body. Fiber optics are also used for telephone and television communication and for the transmission of data in computer systems.

Light can pass through curved tubes. These tubes break the light's path into short tracks that are always straight.

Refraction

You have probably noticed that when people are up to their knees in water, their legs look short and fat. Perhaps you have also looked through a goldfish bowl at a particular angle and seen two fish instead of one. Or, riding along in a car on a sweltering hot day, you may have noticed how the road looks steamy, even though it is perfectly dry. All these things are tricks of light, because of the way it bends when it moves through different materials. The next experiments will show you how light, passing from the air to water and vice versa, changes speed and direction, producing strange visual effects. You will also discover how, by bending the path of light, we can bring closer and enlarge images of objects that are at great distances, such as the Moon.

Why does water change the image of objects?

BENDING LIGHT

You need:
- a glass
- water
- a few drops of milk
- drinking straw
- flashlight
- darkened room

What to do:

1 Fill the glass with water. Add a little milk to make it cloudy.

2 In a darkened room, switch on the flashlight. Shine the beam of light from the top to the bottom so that it shines at an angle on the surface of the water.

What happens?
When the beam of light enters the water, it changes direction.

Misleading depths
Seas, lakes, and rivers often appear less deep than they really are because refraction makes the bottom seem nearer. You only have to try picking up an object from under the water to realize that it is always a little deeper than we think. Fishers who use harpoons never aim at fish where their eyes see them, but at a point that seems lower in the water.

3 Now fill the glass with clean water. Put in the straw.

What happens?
The straw seems to be broken at the point where it enters the water.

Why?
When light passes from air to water, from one transparent substance to another, it changes speed. This, in turn, causes a change in direction. We call this change *refraction*. Refraction can make an object appear to be in a different position than it really is. That is why the part of the straw that is underwater looks as if it has moved away from the part above the water.

Mirages
Rays of light can also undergo a change as they pass from cold air to hot air and vice versa, because these have a different density. (Hot air is less dense than cold air.) Therefore the light passes through at different speeds. On very hot days, the air near the ground gets hot quickly, so the rays that pass through this hot air become crooked. That is why at a distance a street appears to be steamy on a hot day; what we see, in fact, is a reflected image of the sky. In the desert, this effect can cause a mirage—an illusion in which a distant object appears to be nearby.

Light moving through water changes the appearance of objects by the effect of refraction.

How do lenses work?

ENLARGED BY WATER

You need:
- round, glass jar
- paper with a pattern on it
- drinking straw
- water

What to do:

1 Fill the jar with water. Put the straw in it, holding it up straight. Look carefully at the top of the water.

What happens?
The part of the straw that is in the water looks larger.

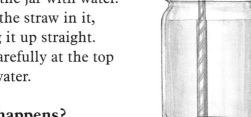

2 Take out the straw. Place the paper with the pattern behind the jar. Look through the jar at the paper.

What happens?
The drawing appears to be enlarged.

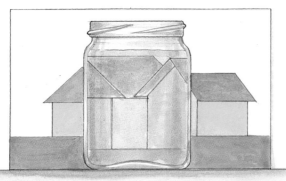

Why?
In the passage from water to air, the rays of light become refracted (change direction). If the surface of separation (for example, the jar or a glass) is curved, refraction makes the object look bigger than it actually is.

RAYS THAT MEET

You need:
- shoe box
- a glass
- water
- flashlight
- pencil
- ruler
- scissors
- darkened room

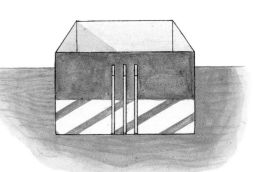

What to do:

1 In a short side of the shoe box, draw and cut three slits 1 cm (0.5 in.) apart.

2 Fill the glass with water and place this in the center of the box, in line with the slits.

3 In the darkened room, switch on the flashlight and shine it onto the slits.

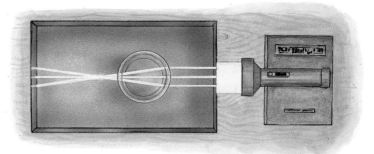

What happens?
Before meeting the glass of water, the rays of light are parallel. But after passing through the glass, they meet at a certain point. (To obtain this effect, you may have to move the glass.) At the point where the rays of light meet, they are stronger.

Why?
The curved surface of the glass and the water causes refraction of the rays of light, making them meet and then cross one another.

UNITING AND SEPARATING LIGHT

You need:
- the shoe box used in the last experiment
- scissors
- convex lens (with the surface curving outward)
- concave lens (with the surface curving inward)
- sheet of white paper
- flashlight
- darkened room

What to do:

1 Cover the bottom of the shoe box with the white paper.

2 With the scissors, make a slit at the bottom of the box into which you can put one of the lenses.

3 Place the convex lens in the slit. In the dark, shine the flashlight at the upright slits.

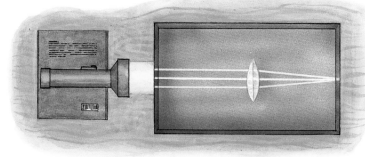

4 Repeat step 3 using the concave lens.

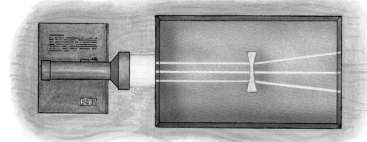

What happens?
The rays that pass through the convex lens change direction and meet at a point. The rays that pass through the concave lens spread out from each other.

Why?
The different shapes of the lenses cause different angles of refraction. Convex lenses bring the rays of light closer together. These lenses can be used to make objects bigger or smaller, depending on the distance of the object from the lens. Concave lenses cause a beam of light to spread out. If a concave lens is put between the eye and an object, it will make the object appear smaller.

Fire
A transparent convex surface, such as the bottom of a bottle, can produce heat as well as concentrate light. Rays from the Sun shining on a bottle thrown away among litter or dry leaves can cause a fire.

Eyeglasses
As you will see in the next pages, there is a lens inside the human eye. This lens enables people to see images both near and at a distance. If the lens does not work properly, vision can be corrected by the use of external lenses—eyeglasses or contact lenses enable near-sighted people to see distant objects better and far-sighted people to see close objects better. They can also make images clearer for people whose eyes cannot focus properly.

Lenses have curved surfaces, so they can make objects appear to be bigger or smaller.

How does a telescope bring an image closer?

THE MOON AT HOME

You need:
- concave mirror
- flat mirror
- magnifying glass
- window

This experiment must be done at night when the Moon can be seen through the window.

What to do:
1. Place the concave mirror in front of the window, turned toward the Moon.

2. Stand in front of the window and slowly turn the flat mirror toward you so that you can see the image of the Moon reflected in the concave mirror. Look through the magnifying glass at the image of the Moon that appears in the flat mirror.

What happens?
In the flat mirror, the Moon appears to be nearer and you can make the image larger with the magnifying glass.

Why?
The concave mirror reflects and brings nearer the image of the Moon. The flat mirror, not being curved, reflects the image exactly and bounces it back through the magnifying glass. This makes the image larger. Telescopes work in the same way, by using reflection.

Who invented the telescope?

The first instruments to bring distant objects nearer and enlarge them were invented in Holland in 1608 by an optician, Hans Lippershey. A year later, Galileo Galilei came to know about this and decided to try making a telescope to study the night sky. The first of Galileo's telescopes was made of two tubes that slid into each other, with a lens at each end. The larger, convex lens was the *objective* that collected the light, and the smaller, concave lens was the *ocular* through which Galileo made his observations. Using this refractor telescope that enlarged objects up to 30 times, Galileo observed and studied the Moon, the planets, and the stars and made important discoveries about the inner solar system. In 1668 Isaac Newton invented the reflective telescope, adding mirrors to the lenses to produce clearer images. The largest telescopes used for astronomical observation are all reflective.

Later, in 1758, achromatic lenses were invented by John Dolland. These were developed so that colors could be seen more distinctly.

The telescope at the Observatory at Brera in Merate, Italy.

A SIMPLE TELESCOPE

You need:
- two magnifying glasses
- two cardboard tubes of slightly different diameters
- tape

What to do:

1 Slide one tube into the other. Tape a magnifying glass at one end.

2 Look at the Moon through the tubes, with your eye against the taped magnifying glass and holding the second glass at the other end. Make the tube longer and shorter and move the second glass until you get a clear image.

What happens?

Through the taped magnifying glass, you can see a closer image of the Moon, but it is upside down.

Why?

The lens at the end makes the rays of light from the Moon converge and create the image inside the tube. The lens nearest the eye enlarges this image and makes the Moon appear closer. Refractor telescopes work in the same way, but these are much larger in order to show images that are not upside down.

Telescopes and microscopes work by a combination of lenses and mirrors, enabling us to see images that are closer and bigger. The picture to the left shows a modern microscope used for the analysis of blood; to the right, a microscope equipped for the study of minerals.

Telescopes make distant objects appear to be nearer by using lenses or a combination of lenses and mirrors.

Colors

When we come out of the dark into the light, instead of seeing things in black and gray, we see colors. Without light, colors do not exist. But how can light enable us to see them? And how is it that two colors mixed together make a third? Why do the crystal drops of a chandelier cast rainbows on the wall when they catch the light? Why is it that the sky is not always the same color? To answer these questions, we must find out more about light as well as color, and discover which colors we can see and which are hidden.

What color is light?

COLORED SPINNING TOP

You need:
- piece of white cardboard
- short pencil with a sharp point
- protractor
- colored felt-tipped pens
- geometry compass
- scissors

What to do:

1 Set the compass at a 5-cm (2-in.) radius to draw a circle 10 cm (4 in.) in diameter on the cardboard. Cut it out.

2 Using the protractor, divide the cardboard circle into seven equal sections, with each section at about 51°.

3 Color the sections in this order: red, orange, yellow, green, blue, indigo, and violet.

4 Thread the pencil through the center of the circle, with the point at the bottom.

5 Spin the circle, as if it were a spinning top.

What happens?
While the top is spinning, the colors cannot be picked out. The circle seems almost white.

Why?
With the fast rotation, all of the seven colors that you have used become mixed together, resulting in a whitish color.

Newton's prism
In the second half of the seventeenth century, Isaac Newton discovered that light, when it passes through a prism (a triangular-shaped solid piece of glass), splits up into rays of different colors that are always in the same order and at the same angle to each other. He called this group of colors the color spectrum.

THE COLORS OF THE RAINBOW

You need:
- flashlight
- shallow rectangular container
- plain mirror
- piece of white cardboard
- water

What to do:

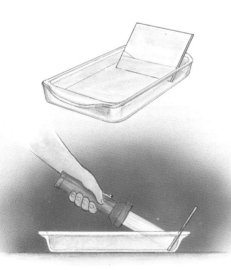

1 Fill the container with water.

2 Put the mirror in the water, and lean it at an angle against a short side of the container.

3 Shine the flashlight on the water so that the beam lights up the part of the mirror that is under water.

4 Place the white cardboard in front of the mirror to catch the reflected light.

What happens?
The white cardboard catches a reflection with the colors of the rainbow.

Why?
The beam of light reflected on the mirror becomes refracted as it escapes from the water. But the colors that make up white light are refracted at different angles, so they fall at different points and become visible.

How a rainbow forms

Tiny drops of water suspended in the air after rain falls work as tiny prisms. As each one is struck by the light, it reflects the light and refracts it, breaking it up into the seven colors of the spectrum.

Light appears to be white, but it is made up of the seven colors of the rainbow, or the color spectrum.

How are colors formed?

COLOR MIXING

You need:
- two flashlights
- two pieces of see-through plastic (one red, one green)
- two rubber bands
- piece of white cardboard
- green, red, yellow, and blue paints
- paintbrush
- plate

What to do:

1 Use the rubber bands to attach a piece of plastic to each flashlight.

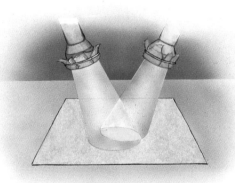

2 Switch on the flashlights. Shine them on the white cardboard, overlapping the two beams of light.

What happens?
The place where the two beams overlap appears yellow.

3 Mix equal quantities of red and green paint on the plate with the brush.

4 Wash out the brush. Then do the same with the yellow and blue paint.

What happens?
Mixing the red and green paint makes a color similar to maroon. The yellow and blue paints make green.

Why?
From the primary colors of sunlight—green, red, and blue—that you mixed two at a time come other colors, called secondary colors. The pigments of primary colors (used in paint, varnishes, and inks) are magenta red, cyan blue (greenish blue), and yellow. From the three primary colors of light, we can make white light; with the three primary color pigments, we can make a very dark color that is almost black.

Toward the end of the nineteenth century, two artists called Signac and Seurat invented the technique of pointillism. Instead of mixing the colors on their palettes, they covered their canvases with tiny little dots of different colors that, seen from a distance, seemed to be fused into one color. You can also try this, perhaps by drawing a meadow with yellow and blue dots close together. From the distance, they will appear green.

How do we see colors?

We can see things around us only if they are illuminated by light rays. But the light that strikes an object is partly absorbed, so it is only partly reflected toward our eyes. The color of an object depends on the color of the light that it reflects. An apple appears red because it reflects only the red color and absorbs all the other colors. White objects reflect almost all of the light, while black objects absorb almost all of the light.

COLORS IN INK

You need:
- bottle of colored ink, or felt-tipped pens of different colors (including black)
- large, flat dish
- water
- strips of white toilet paper, 20 cm (8 in.) long and 2–3 cm (1 in.) wide

What to do:

1 Let one or two drops of ink fall on each strip, at about 2 cm (1 in.) from one end. Or make a dot with one of the felt-tipped pens.

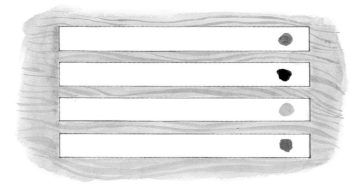

2 Pour a little water into the dish, and dip the very end of each strip (one at a time) into the water. Wait until the water reaches the inky patch.

What happens?
The water gets dirty and some of the dots, including black, break up into different colors.

Why?
The water breaks up the pigment into its separate colors. Each color moves through the wet paper at a different speed. As the colors separate, each one begins to be visible. This experiment will enable you to tell which of the inks and felt-tipped pens are made up of the most colors, and which ones are made up of only one color.

Color on television, color on paper

The images we see on television are made up of tiny lines of the three primary colors of light (red, green, and blue). The eye "mixes" them and sees clear images in all colors. For printing books and magazines, we use the primary pigment colors (yellow, magenta red, and cyan blue), as well as black to make the images more definite. Until recently, each page had to go through the printing machine once for each color. Now one-stage, multi-color printing is common.

By mixing two primary colors together, we make other colors that are called secondary colors.

Can we color white light?

A RED FILTER

You need:
- piece of white paper
- colored felt-tipped pens
- piece of see-through red plastic

What to do:

1 With the felt-tipped pens, make patches of different colors on the paper.

2 Look at all the colors together through the red plastic.

What happens?
The piece of paper appears to be completely red. You will be able to pick out only the brightest patches.

Why?
The plastic acts as a filter. It lets through only the red light and absorbs all the other colors. In the same way, a colored filter placed in front of a spotlight or flashlight blocks out all the colors of white light except its own. So the light that is allowed to pass through is all the same color.

Stained glass windows
Like filters, stained glass lets through only its own colors, keeping us from seeing the others. That is why, when light from the Sun filters through stained glass windows, we see colored reflections on the walls and floor.

When light is colored, the color acts as a filter, blocking out all the colors of the spectrum except its own.

Why does the sky change color?

AN ARTIFICIAL SUNRISE

You need:
- large see-through vase
- water
- milk
- flashlight

What to do:

1 Fill the vase with water. Add a few drops of milk.

2 Switch on the flashlight and shine it down into the water.

What happens?
The water looks bluish.

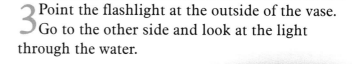

3 Point the flashlight at the outside of the vase. Go to the other side and look at the light through the water.

What happens?
Most of the water takes on a pinkish color while the part that is illuminated appears yellow-orange.

Why?
The water, darkened by the milk, causes a refraction of the colors of light. In the same way, the atmosphere reflects the rays of the Sun, according to its position in relation to Earth.

The colors of the Sun and the sky

When the Sun is high, it appears yellow, and the sky, if it is a calm day, appears blue because the atmosphere filters out all the other colors. At dawn, when the Sun is low, it looks red, and the sky looks pink, red, and yellow. With the rays of light coming at this angle, the colors of the spectrum mix into the atmosphere.

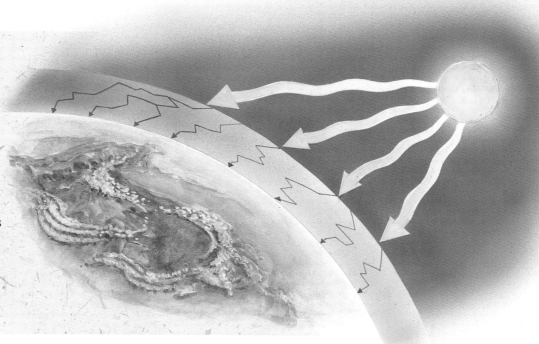

The sky changes color because the atmosphere spreads the light in different ways depending on the position of the Sun.

Why does the color black attract heat?

LIGHT AND HEAT

You need:
- piece of thick aluminum foil
- all-surface black marker
- scissors
- ruler
- tape
- thread
- large, clear glass jar
- piece of strong cardboard, larger than the opening of the jar

What to do:
1 Cut two strips of aluminum foil, each measuring 10 cm × 2.5 cm (4 × 1 in.).

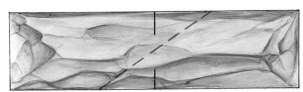

2 With the scissors, cut slits (shown as black lines in the picture).

3 Color one side of each strip black. Then fold as shown by the dashed lines in the picture, so that the black side is inside the fold.

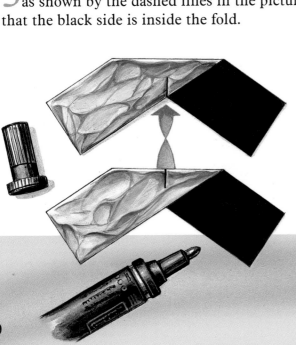

4 Place one strip underneath the other and fasten with tape. Run some thread through the cardboard, as shown in the picture.

5 Hang the strips inside the jar, with the cardboard as a cover. Then put the whole thing in direct sunlight.

What happens?
When the jar has warmed up, the "sails" begin to turn slowly.

Why?
The black sides of the sails absorb more light than the silver sides, which reflect the light. So the black sides get hotter. As they warm the air around them, this warm air spreads out and pushes against the sails, making them turn.

TRAP THE HEAT

You need:
- two glass containers
- water
- piece of black material
- thermometer

What to do:

1 Fill the two containers with water.

2 Cover one container with the black cloth.

3 Put the two containers in direct sunlight and check the temperature each half hour.

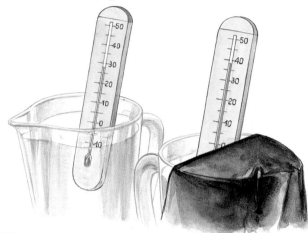

What happens?
The temperature of the water in the jar covered by the black cloth increases more quickly.

Why?
The black cloth almost completely absorbs the light, while the surface of the water reflects it. The light absorbed by the black cloth is transformed into heat. This warms up both the air around the cloth and the water underneath it. That is why wearing black clothes when it is sunny makes us feel hotter than if we were wearing white.

White houses

In very hot countries, houses are painted white to reflect the light. This prevents the intense heat of the Sun from entering the inside of the building.

Black objects almost completely absorb sunlight. Some of this absorbed light is converted into heat.

Capturing an image

For centuries people have searched for ways to record the images of things that they saw around them. Artists made wall paintings, sculptors built statues, artists painted pictures and frescoes. Today we capture images as photographs, movies, television, and videocassettes and keep them to look at. But none of this would be possible if scientists and inventors had not discovered and understood how the human eye works and reproduced this function by mechanical means. From simple boxes in which short-lived images are formed, right up to modern methods of technology that can preserve images, the function of the human eye is always at the beginning of the story.

How does the human eye see?

HOW THE EYE WORKS

You need:
- clear glass bowl (like a goldfish bowl)
- table lamp
- piece of cardboard that is black on both sides
- piece of white cardboard
- scissors
- water
- darkened room

What to do:

1 Fill the bowl with water.

2 Have an adult use the scissors to make a small hole at the center of the black cardboard. Place the cardboard next to the glass bowl.

3 Place the white cardboard on the opposite side, facing the bowl.

4 Darken the room and switch on the table lamp. Line this up in front of the black cardboard so that the beam of light is the same height as the hole.

What happens?
An image of the lamp appears upside down on the cardboard.

Why?
The light from the table lamp enters through the hole of the black cardboard and becomes refracted through the bowl of water, which works like a lens. When the refracted light shines on the white cardboard, it reproduces an image of the lamp, but upside down.

How our eyes work

The pupil in our eye works like the hole in the cardboard. It lets in the light reflected by objects. On the inside of the eye, the light rays meet the lens (represented in the experiment by the bowl full of water), which brings the rays together. These rays then strike the retina at the back of the eye. The retina is a like a screen on which the image is projected, but smaller and upside down. (In the experiment, the retina is represented by the white cardboard).
Why are the images projected upside down?

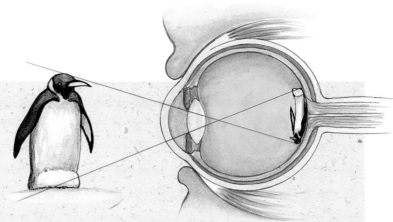

Because the rays of light that enter through the pupil travel in a straight line. As they pass through the lens, they cross over, changing their positions. But our brain reverses the impulses of the optic nerve at the back of the eye so that we see the image correctly.

The images of illuminated objects are projected onto the inside of the eye through the pupil.

How does a camera work?

IMAGES IN A BOX

You need:
- square box without a cover
- cardboard tube
- magnifying glass
- piece of tracing paper
- scissors
- tape
- black paint
- paintbrush
- pencil

What to do:

1 Paint the box black and allow it to dry.

2 Draw around the tube to make a circle on the base of the box. Cut inside the pencil line with scissors. Push the tube into the box.

3 Use the tape to attach the tracing paper over the open end of the box, in place of a cover.

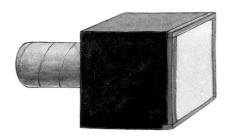

4 Tape the magnifying glass at the opening of the cardboard tube.

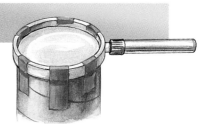

5 Aim the whole thing toward an object that is in good light. Keep the end of the tube with the lens pointed at the object, and the part with the tracing paper towards you.

What happens?
On the tracing paper, you see an image of the object, but it is small and upside down. (You will be able to make the image clearer by moving the tube.)

Why?
The magnifying glass, which is convex, makes the rays of light converge on the inside of the box. The rays cross each other and form an upside-down image on the tracing paper. Thousands of years ago, before it was discovered that eyes do not give out light, boxes similar to this one were invented, in which the light reflected by an object entered simply through a hole, without a lens. The image of the object reproduced on a sheet of paper was then observed with much wonder.

Photographic equipment

In photographic machines, the light enters through the *objective*. This is a lens that gathers light. It can be more or less convex in order to give a narrower or wider image of the object being photographed. The light passes through the opening for a short time (the time it takes to "click" the shutter), and this makes an impression on the photographic film, which is inside, at the back of the camera. The film is coated with a substance that can record images. These images are revealed only when the film is placed in developing fluid to make a negative, from which a print can be made on paper. Ask an adult to show you the inside of a camera. Make sure that the camera does not have any film inside, or the film will be ruined by the tiniest amount of light getting inside.

Through the camera lens, the image of objects is projected and recorded on photographic film.

Space is dark

When the light from the Sun penetrates a partly darkened room, you may see tiny particles moving about in its rays. These particles of dust are called motes. Just as sunlight illuminates these particles clearly enough to be seen, so light spreads through the air during the hours of daylight, and we see everything that is lit up by the Sun. Models of the solar system show the planets wrapped in darkness because in space there is no atmosphere to reflect and spread the rays of the Sun. The planets break up the darkness only when their surfaces reflect light from the Sun. The Moon, Earth's only satellite, also reflects light from the Sun.

The ability of the archerfish

Malay people call this fish the "blowpipe fish." Although the archerfish is only 20 cm (8 in.) long, it has an amazing ability. Without coming above the surface of the water, it can shoot jets of water from its mouth and hit insects that live near the water. Even though they may be up to 1.5 m (5 ft.) above the water, these insects still become easy prey for the archerfish. What is even more extraordinary is that the archerfish, as it takes aim, has to allow for refraction of the light, which makes insects seem to be in a different place from where they really are!

Day and night

Earth rotates on its own axis. This movement of rotation lasts 24 hours (one day) and causes the alternation of day (hours of light) and night (hours of darkness) on different parts of Earth's surface. The length of day and night vary during the year, because, as Earth travels around the Sun during the course of one year, the position of Earth's axis changes in relation to the Sun. In spring and autumn, when the axis is perpendicular to the rays of the Sun, day and night last about the same time. At the beginning of summer, when the North Pole is turned toward the Sun, in the northern hemisphere (the part of the globe north of the Equator) day lasts far longer than night; while in the southern hemisphere (south of the Equator) night is much longer than day. When the South Pole is nearer to the Sun at the beginning of winter, in the southern hemisphere day lasts longer than that in the northern hemisphere, where night lasts longer than day. The difference between the length of day and night is greatest at the North Pole and at the South Pole.

Curved mirrors

The curve of a mirror distorts an image because it changes the angle of reflection of the rays of light. Try to look at yourself in a shiny spoon, first on the inside (concave) and then on the outside (convex). Move the spoon away from yourself, then bring it closer. You will see your reflection changing until it turns upside down. Because of this characteristic, curved mirrors can be used for many purposes. Convex mirrors make images smaller but gather together a greater number of light rays. So a convex car mirror gives the driver a wider view of the road behind the car. Concave mirrors enlarge the image, so they are useful for tasks like applying makeup or shaving.

Metric Conversion Table

When you know:	Multiply by:	To find:
inches (in.)	2.54	centimeters (cm)
feet (ft.)	0.3048	meters (m)
yards (yd.)	0.9144	meters (m)
miles (mi.)	1.609	kilometers (km)
square feet (sq. ft.)	0.093	square meters (m^2)
square miles (sq. mi.)	2.59	square kilometers (km^2)
acres	0.405	hectares (ha)
quarts (qt.)	0.946	liters (l)
gallons (gal.)	3.785	liters (l)
ounces (oz.)	28.35	grams (g)
pounds (lb.)	0.454	kilograms (kg)
tons	0.907	metric tons (t)

To convert degrees Fahrenheit (°F) to degrees Celsius (°C), subtract 32, then multiply by $\frac{5}{9}$.

Glossary

color: the effect that light rays of different wavelengths have on the eyes

concave lens: a type of lens that bends parallel light rays outward. Objects viewed through a concave lens appear smaller.

convex lens: a type of lens that bends parallel light rays so that they meet at a point called the focus. Objects viewed through a convex lens appear bigger or smaller depending on the distance of the object from the lens.

fiber optics: very thin glass or plastic filaments through which light passes

laser: an instrument that produces a narrow, intense beam of light

light: the form of energy that acts on the eye so that one can see

lunar eclipse: an event in which Earth comes between the Sun and the Moon, blocking all or part of the Moon's light

mirage: an image caused by the reflection of light in such a way that a distant object appears to be near

opaque: blocking the passage of light

penumbra: a shadow that is not completely dark

periscope: a tube with mirrors or prisms at each end so that a person can look in one end and see the reflection of an object at the other end

prism: a clear glass or plastic shape that breaks white light into the colors of the spectrum

rainbow: an arc of different colors caused by the bending of sunlight as it passes through drops of water in the air

reflection: rays of light changing direction when hitting a smooth surface

refraction: the bending of light as it passes from one material to another

solar eclipse: an event in which the Moon comes between Earth and the Sun, blocking all or part of the Sun's light

spectrum: the range of colors that is seen when light passes through a prism or a drop of water

sundial: an instrument that shows the time by using the Sun's light. The sundial's pointer casts a shadow across a dial marked in hours.

total internal reflection: the constant reflection of light within an object

translucent: not completely clear, but allowing some light to pass through

transparent: allowing light to pass through so that objects on the other side can be seen clearly

umbra: the darkest part of a shadow

For Further Reading

Asimov, Isaac. *Asimov's Chronology of Science and Discovery.* New York: HarperCollins, 1994.

Burnie, David. *Eyewitness: Light.* London: DK Publishing, 2000.

DiSpezio, Michael Anthony. *Awesome Experiments in Light & Sound.* New York: Sterling Publications, 1999.

Fleisher, Paul. *Matter and Energy.* Minneapolis: Lerner Publications Company, 2002.

———. *Waves.* Minneapolis: Lerner Publications Company, 2002.

Gardner, Robert. *Science Projects About Light.* Berkeley Heights, NJ: Enslow Publishers, Inc., 1994.

Wood, Robert W. *Light FUNdamentals.* New York: McGraw-Hill Professional Publishing, 1996.

———. *Who?: Famous Experiments for the Young Scientist.* Philadelphia: Chelsea House Publishers, 1999.

Websites

Cool Science, sponsored by the U.S. Department of Energy
<http://www.fetc.doe.gov/coolscience/index.html>

The Franklin Institute Science Museum online
<http://www.fi.edu/tfi/welcome.html>

NPR's *Sounds Like Science* site
<http://www.npr.org/programs/science>

PBS's *A Science Odyssey* site
<http://www.pbs.org/wgbh/aso>

Science Learning Network
<http://www.sln.org>

Science Museum of Minnesota
<http://www.smm.org>

Index

About the Author

Antonella Meiani is an elementary schoolteacher in Milan, Italy. She has written several books and has worked as a consultant for many publishing houses. With this series, she hopes to offer readers the opportunity to have fun with science, to satisfy their curiosity, and to learn essential concepts through the simple joy of experimentation.

Photo Acknowledgments

The photographs in this book are reproduced by permission of: Pidello, G., 5; Tessore, A., 6; Liaci, P., 11; Carfagna, G., 12–13; Archivio IGDA, 16, 22, 26–27, 35a; Rizzi, A., 17m, 23b; Castiglioni, A. e.A., 19; Castano, P., 24–25; Laura Ronchi, 25a, 35d; Romano, L., 28; Prato, S., 30–31; Farabolafoto, Ba32; Dani, C., 35b; Buss, W., 35c; front cover: Todd Strand/Independent Picture Service; back cover: Corbis Royalty Free Images

Illustrations by Pier Giorgio Citterio.